LIGHTNING BOLT BOOKS™

Can You Tell a Bee from a Wasp?

Buffy Silverman

Lerner Publications Company
Minneapolis

To Jeff,
my honeybee
—B.S.

Lerner Publications Company
A division of Lerner Publishing Group, Inc.
241 First Avenue North
Minneapolis, MN 55401 U.S.A.

Website address: www.lernerbooks.com

Library of Congress Cataloging-in-Publication Data

Silverman, Buffy.
        Can you tell a bee from a wasp? / by Buffy Silverman.
            p.   cm. — (Lightning bolt books™—Animal look-alikes)
        Includes index.
        ISBN 978-0-7613-6730-7 (lib. bdg. : alk. paper)
        1. Bees—Juvenile literature. 2. Wasps—Juvenile literature. I. Title.
        QL565.2.S52 2012
        595.79—dc22   2010052813

Manufactured in the United States of America
1 — CG — 7/15/11

Contents

Fuzzy or Smooth?

Bees and wasps look a lot alike. Most are yellow and black. You can see through their wings.

Bees (left) and wasps (right) look similar. Can you spot the differences?

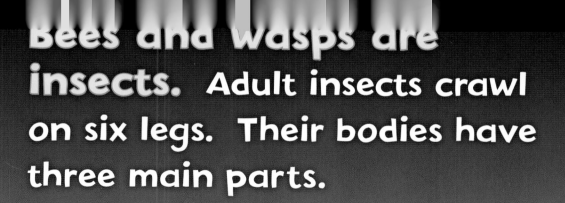

Bees and wasps are insects. Adult insects crawl on six legs. Their bodies have three main parts.

But you can tell them apart. Look at this bee's body. Plump, hairy bodies help bees collect pollen. **Pollen is a powder that flowers make.** It sticks to the bee's hairs.

A bee's back legs are flat.
Female bees have pollen
baskets on their back legs.

A honeybee's pollen basket is a smooth spot on each back leg. Hairs around the basket hold pollen in place.

This wasp's body has no hair. Skinny, smooth bodies let wasps move fast.

A wasp's legs look like thin tubes. They do not have pollen baskets.

Bees and wasps can be colors other than yellow and black. This paper wasp has a red body with thin yellow and black legs.

Finding Food

A bumblebee queen lands on a flower. She drinks a sweet liquid called nectar. Pollen sticks to her furry body. She pushes the pollen into her pollen baskets. Nectar and pollen are food for bees.

The queen is the largest bee in a nest. She lays all the eggs for a nest.

A honeybee flies to her hive. She unloads pollen from her baskets. The queen has laid eggs in the hive. The eggs hatch into larvas. Larvas are young bees that look like worms. They will eat the pollen in the hive.

After the eggs hatch, bees care for the larvas. The larvas look like white worms inside the hive.

A wasp crawls on leaves. She grabs a caterpillar. Wasps are hunters. They catch insects and spiders for their young.

A wasp kills a caterpillar. She will bring the caterpillar to the nest to feed the young.

The wasp flies to her nest. She mashes the caterpillar. She feeds it to wasp larvas. Adult wasps sip nectar from flowers for food. They also drink a sweet liquid that the larvas make.

This wasp chews a caterpillar into mush to feed to larvas.

Living in Groups

Some bees and wasps live in groups. These groups have different kinds of homes.

This nest is home to a group of wasps.

Honeybees live in a hive. Inside are wax cells. Worker bees fill some cells with pollen and honey. They raise young bees in other cells.

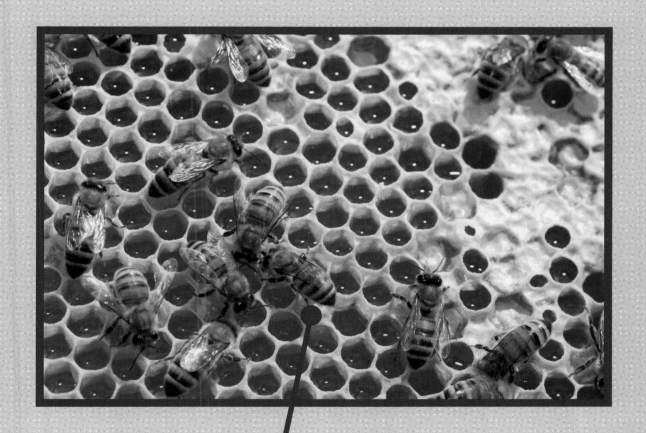

Most of these honeybees are workers. Workers clean the nest. They find food. They care for larvas.

Bumblebees live in underground nests. They make wax pots. Workers store pollen and nectar in them. The queen lays eggs in wax cells.

Bumblebees care for young in a nest in the ground.

Bald-faced hornets live in this nest. Hornets are a kind of wasp.

Wasps build paper nests. Their nests hang from trees or buildings. Wasps chew up twigs or boards. They mix wood with spit to make paper for the nest. They cannot make wax.

Living Alone

Many bees and wasps live alone. No one helps when an egg hatches. The young larva grows up alone. It feeds itself. Young bees and wasps grow up in different places. They eat different foods.

A bee tends to a hole in the ground where she will lay her eggs.

A pollen ball sits at the bottom of a bee's tunnel in the sand.

A bee mother digs a tunnel before she lays eggs. Inside, the bee makes balls of pollen and nectar. She lays an egg on top of each ball. When the larva hatches, it eats the ball.

A potter wasp makes a mud nest. The nest looks like a tiny pot. The mother wasp stings caterpillars. The caterpillars cannot move. The wasp stuffs them into the nest. She lays one egg and flies away. The larva will eat caterpillars.

A potter wasp places a caterpillar in its nest for its larva.

Some wasps have a long tail. It looks like a giant stinger. But it is for laying eggs. This wasp lays eggs inside a caterpillar. Larvas grow inside the caterpillar. They eat the caterpillar.

This wasp has stuck its sharp tail into a caterpillar to lay eggs in it.

Keeping Safe

Many wasps and bees have a tail that can sting. Only females have stingers. Bees use their stingers to protect their home. So do wasps. Wasps also use their stingers when they are hunting.

This close-up photo shows a bee's stinger. The pointy ridges on the side are called barbs.

A honeybee's stinger has big barbs. These sharp points get stuck in skin. So the stinger is ripped from the bee when she flies away. She can only sting once. A honeybee dies while keeping her hive safe.

This honeybee's stinger is pulled away from its body after a sting.

Other bees and wasps have stingers that don't get stuck in skin. A wasp's stinger has tiny barbs. She pulls her stinger out and uses it again. She can sting many times to protect her nest.

The stinger from a yellow jacket wasp looks smooth. Its small barbs won't get stuck in skin.

A spider wasp uses her stinger to poison a spider. She drags the spider to her nest. Then she lays an egg on it. Her larva eats the spider.

A spider wasp mother laid her egg on this spider. The larva eats the spider after it hatches.

Some wasps are more likely to sting people than bees are. In the fall, yellow jackets buzz around people and sweet foods at picnics. They may sting if they are bothered or if they feel in danger.

Watch for bees and wasps in fields and gardens. Can you tell these look-alikes apart?

Who Am I?

Look at the pictures below. Which ones are bees? Which ones are wasps?

 My plump body is covered with hair.

My skinny body is smooth.

 I catch insects and spiders.

I gather pollen and nectar.

 My legs look like tubes.

My back legs are flat. They hold pollen.

Fun Facts

- Cicada killers are a kind of wasp. They sting insects called cicadas and drag them to their nests. A cicada can weigh six times as much as a cicada killer.

- A carpenter bee tunnels through wood. She divides her tunnel into rooms. She puts pollen and nectar in each room. She lays an egg. Adult bees burrow out the next spring.

- A honeybee queen lives three or four years. When she is sick, workers feed larvas a special food. That makes them grow into new queens.

- In the fall, wasp workers raise new queens. Then the workers die. In the spring, new queens start new nests.

Glossary

insect: an animal that has six legs and three main body parts as an adult

larva: a young insect that looks like a worm. A larva is in the stage of its life when it eats and grows.

nectar: a sweet liquid that flowers make

pollen: a powdery material that flowers make. Pollen joins with flower eggs to make seeds.

pollen basket: the part of a bee's hind legs that holds pollen

queen: a female bee or wasp that lays eggs

stinger: a sharp point on a bee or a wasp that can pierce through surfaces and pump poison

worker: a female bee or wasp that protects and cares for others in her nest

Further Reading

Honeybee Printout
http://www.enchantedlearning.com/subjects/
insects/bee/Honeybeecoloring.shtml

Mortensen, Lori. *In the Trees, Honeybees.* Nevada City, CA: Dawn Publications, 2009.

National Geographic Animal Video: Wasp Attacks Spider
http://video.nationalgeographic.com/video/player/
animals/bugs-animals/bees-and-wasps/wasp_
attacks_spider.html

National Geographic Kids Creature Features: Honeybees
http://kids.nationalgeographic.com/kids/animals/
creaturefeature/honeybees

Van Dyck, Sara. *Bumblebees.* Minneapolis: Lerner Publications Company, 2005.

Wasp Printout
http://www.enchantedlearning.
com/subjects/insects/wasp/
Wasp.shtml

Index

Photo Acknowledgments

The images in this book are used with the permission of: © F1 Online/SuperStock, pp. 1 (left), 15; © Belinda Images/SuperStock, p. 1 (right); © James P. Rowan, p. 2; © Tomo Jesenicnik/Dreamstime.com, p. 4 (left); © Frank Greenaway/Dorling Kindersley/Getty Images, pp. 4 (right), 30; © James Urbach/SuperStock, pp. 5, 31; © David Wrobel/Visuals Unlimited, Inc., pp. 6, 28 (top left); © Flirt/SuperStock, pp. 7, 28 (bottom right); © imagebroker.net/SuperStock, pp. 8, 28 (top right); © IndexStock/SuperStock, pp. 9, 28 (bottom left); © Michael Durham/Minden Pictures, p. 10; © Stephen Dalton/Minden Pictures, p. 11; © Vasiliy Vishnevskiy/Dreamstime .com, pp. 12, 28 (middle left); © Premaphotos/naturepl.com, pp. 13, 20, 25; © age fotostock/SuperStock, pp. 14, 27 (both), 28 (middle right); © John B. Free/naturepl.com, p. 16; © Gerry Lemmo, p. 17; © Dwight Kuhn, p. 18; © Dr. John Alcock/Visuals Unlimited, Inc., p. 19; © Albert Mans/Minden Pictures, p. 21; © Ted Kinsman/Photo Researchers, Inc., p. 22; © John B. Free/Minden Pictures, p. 23; © Dr. Dennis Kunkel Microscopy, Inc./Visuals Unlimited, Inc., p. 24; © O. Diez/Arco Images GmbH/Alamy, p. 26.

Front cover: © Aleksander Jocic/Dreamstime.com (both).

Main body text set in Johann Light 30/36.